To

From

Date

Anthony DeStefano

All This and Heaven Too!

HARVEST HOUSE PUBLISHERS
EUGENE, OREGON

Cover photo © iStockPhoto. Interior photos © AdobeStock.
Interior and cover design by Left Coast Design

All This and Heaven Too!

Published by Harvest House Publishers
Eugene, Oregon 97408
www.harvesthousepublishers.com

ISBN 978-0-7369-6475-3 (hardcover)

Library of Congress Cataloging-in-Publication Data

Names: DeStefano, Anthony, author.
Title: All this and heaven too! / Anthony DeStefano.
Description: Eugene : Harvest House Publishers, 2018.
Identifiers: LCCN 2018012853 (print) | LCCN 2018021182 (ebook) | ISBN 9780736964760 (ebook) | ISBN 9780736964753 (hardcover)
Subjects: LCSH: Gratitude—Religious aspects—Christianity.
Classification: LCC BV4647.G8 (ebook) | LCC BV4647.G8 D47 2018 (print) | DDC 242—dc23
LC record available at https://lccn.loc.gov/2018012853

Printed in China
18 19 20 21 22 23 24 25 26 / LP / 10 9 8 7 6 5 4 3 2 1

To my mother,
Laura DeStefano,
to whom I'm grateful for so many things—
especially the gift of life.

Here I am complaining again. Thinking about all the things that are wrong with my life.

But I need to stop right now!

Because the truth is, I just can't believe all the blessings I have.

To start with, I'm alive!
I'm not some rock or piece of clay.

I'm a human being
with an immortal soul.

I'm not some snail
or slimy slug.

And even though I'm not in the best shape in the world,
I'm still breathing and moving and living.

And even though I don't have enough money to dine at fancy restaurants all the time, I always have enough to eat.

And even though the place I live feels small and cramped, I'm lucky to have a roof over my head.

And even though I don't always agree with the government, I'm grateful to live in this country. With all its problems, God bless America!

Yes, I'm grateful for so many
things—like my family.

And my relatives from the past, who made my existence possible…

And my friends…

And the many strangers who have
showed me kindness when I needed it.

And, of course, my beloved pet!

Yes, it's true I may not lead the most exciting life,
but there are still so many simple and wonderful
things to do—like going for long drives.

And cooking tasty meals…

And painting pretty pictures…

And taking soothing baths.

There are so many beautiful things to see,
too—like the wonders of nature.

And sparkling city skylines…

And fireflies at twilight…

And the starry night.

There are so many beautiful things
to smell, too—like wood smoke.

And freshly
brewed coffee…

And baked breads and pies...

And fragrant flowers…

And salty ocean breezes.

There are so many beautiful sounds
to hear, too—like music playing.

And people laughing…

And birds chirping…

And the simple silence
of a snowy night.

I'm also grateful for all the things
I CAN'T see with my eyes—like love.

And honor…

And loyalty…

And duty…

And courage…

And God's angels, and
the whole world of the spirit.

I'm grateful that even though God sometimes seems distant, He's really not.

He's right here! I can have a deep relationship with Him—through prayer.

And His Word…

And the life of His church.

I'm grateful that God is always with me.
Even when everyone else abandons me,
I'll never be alone as long as I believe.

I'm grateful that even though I keep messing up,
God always forgives me when I'm sorry.

I'm grateful that even when I feel overwhelmed by stress, I can have a deep inner peace that the Bible says "transcends all understanding."

I'm grateful that even when I feel weak and small,
I have supernatural power to overcome all my problems
—because nothing is impossible with God.

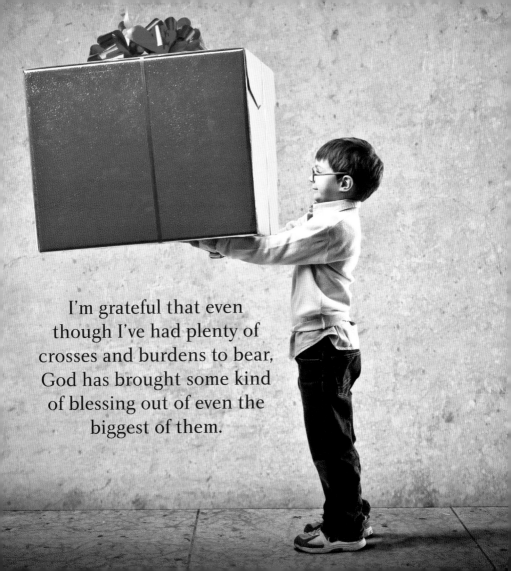

I'm grateful that even though I've had plenty of crosses and burdens to bear, God has brought some kind of blessing out of even the biggest of them.

I'm grateful that God has given me a unique destiny, planned from all eternity—a special pathway for me to take, a door in the universe only I can unlock.

Most of all, I'm grateful that God loves
me so much that He died for me.

And even though I'm sad when I think of my
family and friends who have passed on, I know
they're not really gone. They're waiting for
me right now on the other side…

And one day I'll be able to kiss and hug them and
hear their voices and talk to them again!

One day I'll be able to live with them in the next world—a world that will be even more colorful and filled with joy and adventure than this one—a whole new creation!

A world where I'll be able to see God face-to-face…

A world where there will be
no more sadness or suffering…

A world where
I'll be young and
strong forever.

That's why even though I get depressed sometimes and feel like complaining, I know that when it comes to God's blessings, I'm already rich—in fact, I'm a billionaire.

So yes, Lord, I'm very grateful for all this…

And Heaven too!!

Give Thanks to the Lord

Give thanks to the LORD, for he
is good; his love endures forever.

—1 CHRONICLES 16:34

Rejoice always, pray continually, give
thanks in all circumstances; for this is
God's will for you in Christ Jesus.

—1 THESSALONIANS 5:16-18

Do not be anxious about anything, but in every
situation, by prayer and petition, with thanksgiving,
present your requests to God. And the peace of God,
which transcends all understanding, will guard
your hearts and your minds in Christ Jesus.

—PHILIPPIANS 4:6-7